SABRINA FISHER REECE

When I say "I AM "

How the "I AM" Statement Can Change Your Life

9in59Seconds Publishing Co.

Contents

1

When I Say I Am

How your spoken identity activates spiritual and universal law.

When I say **"I Am,"** I am not merely forming words with my mouth, I am issuing a declaration to the universe. I am speaking into existence the identity I choose to wear, the reality I am willing to claim, and the direction my life will follow. **"I Am"** is not passive language. It is an act of creation. It is the moment thought becomes sound, and sound becomes substance. Long before a result ever appears in the physical world, it is first spoken into being through the vibration of these two words. It's not New Age, it's not old school religion, it is simple fact. The words we speak about ourselves become our reality.

Every time you say **"I Am,"** something inside of you listens. Your spirit listens. Your subconscious listens. Even your body listens. These words carry authority because they are rooted in identity. Who do you believe you are? You are not describing a future possibility when you speak **"I Am."** You are stating a truth that your mind, your spirit, and your actions immediately begin working to fulfill. This is why careless **"I Am"** statements can quietly sabotage a life, while intentional ones can rebuild it from the inside out.

Most people say **"I Am"** without realizing the weight of what they are declaring. "I **Am** tired." "I **Am** broke." "I **Am** unlucky." "I am not enough." Spoken repeatedly, these phrases do not remain harmless expressions of emotion. They become instructions. They become seeds. The mind accepts them as factual. The body responds as though they are law. Over time, life begins to mirror what has been spoken, not because the words were true at first, but because belief gave them permission to become true.

For example: We utter phrases like: **I Am** tired, **I Am** dumb, **I Am** old all the time. I realize that the logical brain will tell you that what you are saying is true. However the amazing power that God gave you to create a great life for yourself is not logical. It is spiritual and words and thought begin designing your life in the spiritual realm long before you see anything in the physical realm.

The power of **"I Am"** is ancient. It is woven into the fabric of creation itself. In sacred scripture, God reveals Himself not through limitation or explanation, but through identity. When Moses stood before the burning bush and asked who was sending him, God did not give a description. God gave a declaration: **"I Am That I Am."** This was not merely a name, it was a revelation of eternal being, self-existence, and divine authority. It was God revealing Himself as the source of all identity, all power, all existence, and all becoming.

When you speak **"I Am,"** you are not claiming divinity, but you are mirroring the law of identity that was established at the foundation of creation. You are stepping into the spiritual law that precedes outcome. You are exercising the human portion of a divine principle: What is spoken with authority begins to exist with structure. This is why Scripture repeatedly shows God speaking before things appear: "Let there be light." And then there was light. Speech preceded manifestation. Declaration preceded form. The Kingdom of Heaven is within us all. Through our God-given power we can command the life we desire but we must begin with speaking exactly who we choose to be, not what reality is presenting at the moment. Speak life, love, happiness, peace, prosperity and abundance into your life by using the "**I Am**" statement.

Long before I finished my first book I learned the importance of speaking success into my career as an author. I spoke phrases like: "I Am a best selling author of many books" and it soon became my reality. That same tool is available to us all.

Your life is constantly moving in the direction of the strongest identity you hold about yourself. It is not driven solely by what you want, but by who you believe you are. If you believe you are powerful, your decisions will reflect confidence. If you believe you are broken, your choices will reflect fear. If you believe you are blessed, your spirit will search for opportunity even in difficult seasons. "**I Am**" statements are the bridge between inner belief and outer experience.

What you declare consistently becomes what you stand on unconsciously. Over time, your language becomes your posture. It shapes how you walk into rooms, how you approach relationships, how you pray, how you expect, how you believe, how you endure challenges, and how you receive blessings. Long before circumstances shift, identity must shift. And identity is most directly shaped through what you say about yourself when no one is correcting you.

Jesus later reinforced this same spiritual law when He said, *"According to your faith, let it be done unto you."* Faith is not just belief, it is spoken agreement. What you speak consistently is what you place faith in. You may not even be consciously aware that you are forming subconscious beliefs with your words but you are.

What you place faith in is what you authorize to grow in your life. You cannot continually speak defeat and expect victory to feel safe entering your world. You cannot continually speak lack and expect abundance to feel invited. You can change you entire life by changing the words you chose to speak.

To master your life, you must first master your **"I Am"** statements. You must become deliberate with the way you label yourself in moments of emotion, pressure, and uncertainty. The goal is not to deny what you feel, but to avoid imprisoning yourself with permanent labels attached to temporary conditions. You can acknowledge pain without declaring yourself powerless. You can admit exhaustion without declaring yourself defeated. The language you choose becomes the agreement you live under. So often we casually use phrases like "These knees are giving out on me" or "My memory is failing me." Train yourself to view situations like those as temporary. Do not speak of them as permanent fact.

When you say **"I Am,"** you are either agreeing with limitation or aligning with possibility. and as I say in all my books "All Things Are Possible". Even when what you are attempting to accomplish seems challenging, watch your words. Do not give in to phrases like these:

"**I Am** not capable of this"

   "**I Am** not as smart as you think"

   "**I Am** not going to finish school"

   "**I Am** not going to fine the job I want.

When using the **I Am** statement you are either reinforcing the past or calling forth the future. These two words sit at the doorway between who you have been and who you are becoming. They carry the power to anchor you in negative cycles or elevate you into transformation.

Throughout Scripture, we see God repeatedly renaming people before their lives change. Abram became Abraham. Sarai became Sarah. Simon became Peter. Jacob became Israel. Their names were redefined before their destinies unfolded. God was shifting identity before He shifted circumstance. This is the same pattern at work in your life today. What you call yourself today determines what your future feels permitted to become.

This chapter is an invitation to listen closely to your own voice. To become aware of the quiet declarations you speak over yourself every day. Because before the world ever calls you anything, you have already named yourself through your own words. When you say "**I Am**," you are not just describing your life. You are shaping it.

Daily "I AM" Affirmations – Speak This Into Your Life

This page is not meant to be read once. It is meant to be used. Return to it daily. Stand in front of a mirror. Place your hand over your heart. Breathe deeply. Then speak these words slowly, with intention and belief. Your life responds to agreement. The first set of **I Am** affirmations are basic and simple:

I Am Happy

   I Am Smart

   I Am Safe

   I Am Kind

   I Am Focused

   I Am Healthy

   I Am Successful

   I Am Loved

   I Am Peaceful

You must cover the basics first then move on to the more detailed I Am statements

I Am divinely created.

   I Am guided by wisdom greater than my own.

   I Am learning to trust myself and God more each day.

   I Am releasing fear and choosing faith.

   I Am worthy of love, peace, and abundance.

   I Am becoming stronger in every way.

   I Am aligned with purpose and divine timing.

   I Am open to growth and transformation.

   I Am protected, supported, and provided for.

   I Am walking forward with confidence.

Now pause. Feel those words settle. Then begin writing your own declarations below. These are your personal agreements with the life you are creating.

Write Your Daily "I AM" Declarations:

I Am _____

_____

I Am _____

_____

I Am _____

_____

I Am _____

_____

I Am _____

_____

I Am _____

_____

I Am _____

_____

I Am _____

I Am _____

_____

I Am _____

_____

Daily Instruction for the Reader

Speak your "**I AM**" statements out loud every morning before you begin your day.

Speak them again at night before you go to sleep.

Speak them when fear tries to rename you.

Speak them when doubt feels louder than faith.

Speak them until belief replaces hesitation.

Speak them until behavior begins to shift.

Speak them until they feel natural.

Speak them until your life begins to agree.

I suggest recording them in your own voice on your cell phone and playing them when you are driving, walking or settling down to sleep. Allow them to seep past the conscious mind and seep into the subconscious mind. That is where the magic of manifestation happens.

I created a movement called the #In59Seconds Movement. I know we are all busy but it does not take more than 59 seconds to uplift yourself and speak greatness into your life. Commit to speaking Life, Creativity, Perfect Health and Prosperity into yourself and others daily. Start with a simple 59 seconds. Join the movement and do your part in creating a better world. **#In59Seconds**

2

Your Cells Can Hear you

Your body is not just flesh and bone. It is a living, listening system made up of trillions of intelligent cells, each one responding every moment to the messages it receives. Every word you speak sends instruction not only into the atmosphere around you, but into the microscopic universe within you. Your cells are not deaf to your voice. They hear you. They obey you. And over time, they become what you repeatedly tell them to be.

I have made it a habit to speak the day I desire into existence. When I'm getting into my car I say: *"Thank you God for keeping me covered in your Divine bubble of protection, allowing me to travel to and from my destination safely"*. As I am waking into my salon there is a small, dimly lit foyer, I stop there and say *"Today is a productive day, **I Am** abundance, **I Am** prosperity"*. Notice I did not say *"God can today be productive please?"* I claimed that it already was.

Science now confirms what ancient wisdom has always known: The human body is responsive to vibration. Sound is vibration. Thought is vibration. Emotion is vibration. When you speak, you release a frequency that moves through your nervous system, your bloodstream, your organs, and deep into the structure of your cells. Your biology is constantly interpreting these signals. It does not argue with your words. It accepts them as information. So if you speak negatively the same rule applies. If you say things like "I'll never be happy" or "I'm not good at this" then that will become your reality.

Recently I was walking a client to the door at my salon and I said "Don't forgot to book your next appointment in six weeks." He said "Girl I'm broke." He thought it was funny and was clearly used to impulsively spitting that phrase out of his mouth. I replied "You better knock it off, you know the importance of words." Many of us say a lot of self-sabotaging words regularly, never realizing we are shaping our lives.

Modern medicine now recognizes an entire field called psychoneuroimmunology, which is the study of how thoughts, emotions, and beliefs influence the immune system. Research shows that chronic negative thoughts increase cortisol, the body's primary stress hormone. When cortisol remains elevated for long periods of time, it suppresses immune function, increases inflammation, disrupts sleep, weakens digestion, impairs memory, and accelerates disease. In contrast, sustained positive emotional states have been shown to lower cortisol levels, improve immune responses, and support cellular repair. What you think and speak literally changes the chemical environment inside your body. I understand in a stress filled world, being positive is not always as easy as it seems. However there is truly nothing more important. Monitoring your words and your thought are truly the key to a comfortable, abundant life.

Careless speech is never truly harmless. When you repeatedly say, "**I Am** sick," your cells begin to organize around sickness.

When you say, "**I Am** tired," your body prepares for exhaustion. When you say, "My body is failing," or "My head is killing me," your system receives those words as instruction rather than expression. The subconscious does not recognize exaggeration. It does not know you are being dramatic. It only recognizes repetition. What you speak long enough, your body learns to embody. Speak life and love, peace and prosperity even if it feels like a lie at first. Trust me on this. Speak the positive affirmation representing precisely what you desire in your life and eventually it will become second nature to you. My brain starts reciting positive affirmations even before my body fully wakes up in the morning. Before my feet hit the floor in the morning, my mind had already claimed a great day. I have trained it to do so. This is learned behavior and it takes a minute to become habitual, but it's possible.

Your cells were designed for alignment with life, not destruction. They were created to regenerate, to heal, to renew, to adapt, and to restore balance. But they require direction. Just like a garden requires a specific seed. The cells in our body depend on the signals they receive from the brain, the nervous system, and the voice. When you flood your internal environment with fear-filled language, hopeless statements, or constant declarations of weakness, you interfere with the natural intelligence of your body.

The medical world also recognizes the powerful influence of expectation through what is known as the placebo and nocebo effect. Studies reveal that patients who believe a treatment will help often experience real physiological improvement, even when the treatment contains no active medicine. Their belief alone triggers measurable changes in pain perception, immune response, heart rate, and hormone levels. On the other hand, patients who expect harm often experience negative symptoms even when nothing harmful has been administered. This proves that belief and expectation-formed largely through language-directly influence biological outcomes.

In simple terms, **speak it, believe it, live it.** How many times have we seen political candidates who were far from qualified and cocky as heck, actually win? Their arrogance may annoy others but it allowed then to shift into a place of unshakable belief. The spiritual law does not judge, it complies.

The cells of your body can hear you. They hear every word you say, good or bad. Words are not just heard with the ears. They are processed as instruction on a cellular level. This is why two people can face the same diagnosis and experience completely different outcomes. One speaks life even in uncertainty. The other speaks fear as fact. Their bodies respond accordingly. Healing does not begin only in the medicine cabinet. It begins in the language cabinet. What you say determines what your cells prepare for. the words you speak create the life you live.

Your cells are living witnesses to every declaration you make about yourself. They register your depression. They register your hope. They register your faith. They register your fear. When you speak words filled with stress, your body produces chemicals that mirror that stress.

I remember a friend of mine had a thirteen year old daughter. We were all at an amusement park and I told her I would hold her purse so she could have fun. She said "Oh no Ms. SaBrina I have anxiety really bad and my medicine is in my purse." I felt horrible for this young child that she was indefinitely tethered to this purse for fear of a sudden anxiety attack coming on. Not to down play what some believe are actual medical conditions but she was way to young to have accepted this as her forever fate.

When you speak words filled with peace and expectancy, your body releases chemistry that supports healing and balance. You are not separate from what you say. You become what you say at the deepest physical level.

Epigenetics, something I learned of from watching Greg Braden videos, is the study of how behaviors and environment affect the way genes turn on or off. It has shown us something profound: your genetic blueprint is not your destiny. Your thoughts, language, stress level, emotional state, and environment influence how your genes express themselves. In other words, the words you speak and the emotions you reinforce help decide which internal switches get turned on. Even your DNA responds to your internal language.

So stop here for a second please. Take a deep breath. Turn off all televisions and external stimuli. Continue to breathe deeply and sit in silence for a minute. Now ask yourself "What have I been saying to myself?, What does my internal dialog sound like?" This is the first step. You can not change the words you speak over your life if you have not sat still long enough to hear what they are.

Many people unknowingly program their bodies for breakdown while praying for healing. They ask God for health but constantly speak sickness all day long. They declare recovery in prayer but declare defeat in conversation. The body receives both signals, but it responds most powerfully to the one that is spoken with consistency, emotion, and belief. Your cells take their cues not only from your prayers, but from your everyday language.

This is not about denying reality. It is about choosing authority over it. You can acknowledge symptoms without declaring them as identity. For example: You can say "**I Am** temporarily without funds" as opposed to "**I Am** broke." You can recognize pain without branding yourself as broken. You can be currently experiencing actual physical pain in your knees, without saying "My knees are killing me." You can face uncertainty without sentencing your body to failure. There is a difference between describing what you feel and declaring what you are. Your cells respond to what you claim as truth about yourself.

When you speak strength, your body searches for strength. When you speak healing, your cells begin to organize toward restoration. When you speak life, your body aligns with life. Even when healing is still in process, your words can prepare the environment for recovery. Every "**I Am** getting stronger" carries a different vibration than "**I Am** always sick." One builds the body. The other burdens it. You choose how you use the "**I Am**"statement.

In January 2025 I had major surgery to remove a tumor from my head. The risk were sudden death, stroke, hearing loss and facial paralysis. It was vital the state of mind I chose to be in while entering that surgery. Fortunately I had been at this positive affirmation thing for many years so I got to work even through my fear. I visualized myself the day after the surgery, wide awake looking into a mirror with no facial paralysis. I imagined smiling really hard and feeling grateful. This kept me calm although I was indeed slightly afraid. All I could do was do what I know to be true. Speak it, feel it, visualize it and command it into my life.

I woke up perfect! No complications other than a slight blood pressure spike that kept me there an extra day. But the tumor was removed fully by Dr. Ikera Isihiyama from UCLA Hospital in California, and he does not expect the tumor to return. And it won't, because I will not entertain the thought even one time. If the logical brains starts to put the thought of it in my mind, I will cast out the thought and visual and replace it with a image of me at my 80th birthday party, in perfect health dancing and smiling with my family and friends.

Your nervous system is constantly monitoring your internal dialogue. When your language is dominated by fear, your body remains trapped in survival mode. This keeps adrenaline and cortisol flowing, tightens muscles, restricts digestion, weakens immunity, and exhausts your system. When your language shifts to safety, expectancy, and hope, your body shifts into rest-and-repair mode. Blood flow improves. Digestion stabilizes. Cells repair more efficiently. Healing speeds up. Your words decide which mode your body lives in.

Your voice is not just a communication tool for others. It is a command center for your own biology. Every sentence you speak over yourself is either assisting your body's design or working against it. The tongue is small, but its reach is vast. It touches nerve endings, hormones, immune responses, and the quiet intelligence of every cell that makes you who you are.

If your words have helped create a condition, then your words can participate in the correction of it. This is not fantasy. This is alignment. This is cooperation between your spirit, your mind, and your body. Your cells are alive. They are responsive. They are listening. And they are waiting on your instruction every single day.

You do not have to shout. You do not have to be perfect. You only have to be consistent. Gentle, steady declarations spoken in faith reshape internal chemistry over time. Healing is not always instant, but it is always responsive to agreement.

Speak life to your body, Speak strength to your organs-Speak peace to your nervous system-Speak restoration to your cells-Speak alignment to your DNA. They were created to respond to life.

And they are listening to you now.

3

The Garden You Plant

Understanding how your thoughts become the seeds of your future.

I absolutely love gardening. When I lived in California, I built a beautiful garden in my backyard. I planted and harvested potatoes, strawberries, tomatoes, kale, spinach, cilantro, carrots, cantaloupe, beets, and broccoli. It was one of the most gratifying experiences of my life. I even taught my two youngest daughters how to grow their own food with their own hands. Watching them learn where nourishment truly comes from was pure joy. But as much happiness as home gardening brought me, its significance cannot even compare to the seeds you plant in your mind.

Mind is all. M=Manipulating **I**=Ideas in a **N**=New **D**= Direction.

Your mind is a living garden. Every thought you think is soil being turned. Every word you speak is a seed being dropped. And just like any natural garden, your inner world will always produce according to what is planted there, never according to what you merely wish for. You may desire peace, abundance, love, and health, but if the seeds you consistently plant are fear, lack, resentment, and doubt, the harvest will always reflect the seed, not the desire.

No garden grows by accident. Everything that appears in it is the direct result of what was planted there, what was watered, and what was left untouched. The same is true of the mind and the inner world. Some of what grows in your life today came from seeds you planted years ago without even realizing it. Some came from seeds planted by other people's words that you accepted as truth. But the power to plant anew has always remained in your hands. It's never too late dig up the roots of that old soil and plant new seeds.

Your words are not casual when they hit the soil of your subconscious. They carry life inside them. When you speak, you are sowing. When you repeat, you are watering. When you believe, you are cultivating. Over time, your inner landscape begins to take shape quietly, invisibly, and faithfully. The mind does not question the seed. It nurtures whatever it receives. That is precisely how the subconscious mind works. It will not judge you and tell you that something is not good for you. It will simply produce the exact seeds that you planted.

Many people walk through life wondering why the same cycles keep growing back. They keep harvesting disappointment, instability, poverty and bad relationships, emotional exhaustion without realizing they have been planting the same type of seed with their language, expectations, and inner and outer dialogue. We often ask God to change the harvest while continuing to plant the very seeds that produced it. But harvest does not respond to prayer alone. It responds to what is planted consistently.

The most dangerous seeds are not always loud. Many are whispered daily in private. "Nothing ever works out for me." "I'll never get ahead." "This is just how my life is." These quiet statements sink deep into the soil of the mind and take root. Over time, they grow into belief. And belief grows into lived reality.

But the same soil that grows weeds can grow fruit. The same mind that learned fear can learn faith. The same inner ground that once produced limitation can be replanted with possibility. This is the power of intentional planting. When you begin to choose your words with care, you begin choosing your future with care, and that is the key to a happy life.

You cannot plant corn and expect roses. You cannot plant fear and harvest peace. You cannot speak defeat over your life daily and expect victory to rise naturally out of that soil. Nature responds only to seed. And the mind follows the same divine law of reproduction. What you plant in thought and speech is what multiplies in experience.

This is why transformation does not start with circumstances. It starts with replanting. It starts with pulling up what no longer serves you. It starts with recognizing which words you have been scattering daily and asking yourself honestly what kind of harvest they are designed to produce. It is never to late. No matter how bad you have been treating yourself. No matter what horrible words you have said about yourself. The same way you can go outside and pull up those weeds and turn over that old soil, add new fertilizer and plant something new. You can do that for your life.

You are always gardening, whether you are aware of it or

not. The only difference between a life that flourishes and a life that feels overrun is intention. The gardener who neglects the garden will still grow something, but it will be wild, un-managed weeds, that often have painful thorns. The gardener who tends carefully, consistently, and patiently will see beauty emerge over time. Same concept rather its a fruit and vegetable garden or the garden of your mind. You are the gardener and you are in control.

Your future is quietly growing beneath the surface right now. Every word you speak today is shaping what will be visible tomorrow. You may not see the change immediately. Seeds do not shout when they are planted. But they never forget where they were placed. And in due season, they always rise and flourish.

If you want a different harvest in your life, you must plant different words. If you want happiness, love, great health, prosperity and peace in your life. You must be mindful of the seeds you plant in your mind.

What you seek is seeking you, so if you want peace, speak peace. If you want healing, speak life and great health, even on days when you are feeling bad. If you want abundance, speak expectation. Eliminate thoughts of lack and limitation from your mindset. Your mind will grow what your mouth keeps sowing. The garden never argues. It simply produces. And so does your life. Every repetition of fear strengthens fear's roots. Every repetition of faith strengthens faith's harvest. You are always cultivating something, whether consciously or unconsciously. There is no such thing as neutral soil in the inner world.

The beauty of a garden is that it can always be restored. No matter how long weeds have grown, new planting is never forbidden. The moment you change what you plant, the future quietly begins to shift. Your mind is ready for new seeds. Your life is waiting on what you choose to plant next. The past may explain your soil, but it does not have to control your harvest. What you plant today carries more authority than anything that was planted yesterday.

The "**I Am**" statement is the most powerful seed you can place into your mental garden. Every time you say "**I am** broken," you fertilize pain. Every time you say "**I am** blessed," you invite increase. Every time you say "**I am** tired," you strengthen exhaustion. And every time you say "**I am** strong," you activate endurance. "**I am** wealthy," you activate prosperity. Your identity follows your declarations. The spirit listens. The subconscious listens. The universe responds. The harvest never delays forever, it simply waits for maturity.

Your words do not just describe your reality they systematically **design** it. The blueprint of your future is written in the language you use today. If you continue to speak from the soil of old trauma and pain, you will continue to harvest from it. But if you begin to speak from the soil of happiness, love, faith, expectation, and divine promise, your life must respond accordingly. The seed always obeys the voice that plants it. And you are the gardener of your life.

So choose your words with great respect, love and certainty. Talk to your life as if it is listening, because it is. Speak to your dreams as if they are alive, because they are. Speak to your healing as if it has already begun, because in truth, it already has. Let your mouth agree with what heaven already knows about you.

Today, you stand in your garden with seeds in your hands. The soil is ready. The season is open. What you declare now will become what you experience next. Choose life. Choose love. Choose abundance. And most of all, choose your "**I Am**" wisely, because everything you will ever become is already hidden inside the words you speak.

4

The Power Of Your Words

Why what you speak carries creative, destructive, or healing force.

Your words are not ordinary. They are not just sound. They are not simply communication passed between people. Your words are carriers. They transport belief, expectation, fear, faith, life, and death. Long before a circumstance ever shifts, it first responds to the language it is wrapped in. This is why the words you choose in private matter just as much as the words you speak in public. You are always speaking life into something, even when you think you are just talking. Your words, good or bad will shape the trajectory of your life.

Every season of your life has been shaped by language. Some of it came from what others spoke over you. Some of it came from what you learned to say to yourself. And I can tell you without hesitation that I have been carried, covered, and protected by the prayers spoken over me long before I understood their power.

My beloved grandmother, **Ella Mae Fisher Fair**, was one of the greatest spiritual forces in my life.

She was an amazing woman, strong, gentle, wise, and grounded in her faith. She was originally from Dallas, Texas. She raised me and my older sister, Mary, because life had dealt our parents a difficult hand. Our mother battled drug addiction, and our father, her own son, struggled with alcoholism. In a world that felt unstable, my grandmother became our anchor. She stepped in without hesitation, raising us as her own, pouring love into every crack life had left in us.

She taught us kindness. She taught us values. She taught us what it meant to live with integrity. And most importantly, she taught me how to pray—not as a ritual, not as a performance, but as a lifeline to something greater than myself. Her prayers surrounded me, shaped me, and protected me in ways I didn't understand until I grew older.

And now here I am, standing on the foundation she built, teaching *you* about prayer, not just the prayer that pleads, but the prayer that **creates**. Not just the prayer that hopes, but the prayer that **aligns**. Not just the prayer she taught me, but the *effective* prayer that will reshape your life just as surely as her prayers reshaped mine.

Much of the life you are living now comes from what you have been repeatedly speaking over yourself. You did not arrive at this chapter of your story by accident. You arrived here through a trail of declarations, some intentional, some emotional, some spoken in faith, some spoken in fear. But all of them carried power. All words have power. That's why our elders used to tell us as children, "Watch your mouth" and especially watch the words you speak over your own life.

Your words have weight because they are attached to your beliefs. Often we are first introduced to belief systems through the people who raised us. They taught us what to fear and what to limit. I'm not angry at them, and I don't want you to be either. They meant no harm. I'm simply pointing out that many of our ancestors did not believe abundance was possible. They truly didn't know any better. Yes, being taught to save is a beautiful thing, but it should never be rooted in a mindset of lack. You can prepare for the winter without living in fear of famine. Even a whisper becomes powerful when it is repeated often enough. Craft personal positive affirmations for yourself and speak them aloud repeatedly.

Your inner conversations are just as influential as the words you speak out loud. The life you live externally is always the echo of the language you have agreed with internally. Before you ever stepped into confidence, you rehearsed it in thought. Before you ever felt defeated, you practiced it with words. Long before the outside world responds, your inner world has already voted.

What you consistently tell yourself becomes the agreement your spirit lives under. If you repeatedly say, "I can't," the universe hears permission to block you. If you repeatedly say, "I'm not enough," life will mirror that belief back to you. But when you begin to say, "I am capable," "I **am** worthy," and "**I am** gifted," " **I am** smart," "**I am** healthy," your reality begins re-calibrating itself to match that higher declaration. Language is direction. The very direction needed to design a great life.

You were never meant to inherit the emotional limitations of past generations. You were meant to break those agreements and form new ones rooted in faith, possibility, and divine truth. Your mouth is not just for speaking what you see, it is for calling forth what you choose to become. It is for manifesting the unseen into your current reality. The moment you shift your language, you shift your life's flow, and then you realize you can do all things. The sky becomes the limit.

You never truly rise above what you continually speak beneath your breath. The voice you most often obey is your own. The words you speak over yourself take precedence. If your words are filled with expectancy. If you expect success, greatness, good health, you will walk in every room differently. If your words are filled with doubt, then fear and insecurity will quietly guide your decisions. If your words are hopeful and expansive, then endurance and strength will return even in the middle of delay. Language always becomes instructions to the soul. What are the words you speak to your soul.?

There are moments when life will try to strip your voice of its authority. Hurt and disappointment will get you off track. How we speak when we are hurt is vital to our future. Disappointment happens to us all, it tries to silence our positive "**I Am**" declarations. Trauma tries to re-frame our identity. What seems to be unanswered prayers from God, try to convince us that our words no longer matter. But the truth is, your voice matters most when unfavorable circumstances attempt to challenge you. This is when you are at the height of emotion. This is when your words shift from description to declaration. This is when your mouth becomes a tool of alignment rather than a mirror of emotion. Remember, manifestation requires words spoken with emotion to materialize.

Absolutely — here is an expanded, richer, more connected version that flows beautifully in your voice and adds even more depth about ancient wisdom, early metaphysical teachers, and the lineage of thought that supports your message.

From Neville Goddard to many of the trailblazers before him, the greatest teachers have all echoed the same truth: **the mind is the birthplace of reality.** Neville taught that imagination, feeling, belief, and language are not casual tools, they are creative forces. When aligned, they become the spiritual technology through which your desires move from the invisible realm into physical form. But Neville was only one voice in a vast and ancient choir.

I've always been drawn to the work of early thought leaders like: Les Brown, Zig Ziglar, Neville Goddard—men whose messages still ripple through time. What brings me comfort is realizing that the principles I am teaching in this book are not new revelations. They are ancient truths rediscovered. People from the 1800s and early 1900s understood the necessity of monitoring the mind, disciplining thought, and mastering inner speech.

Take **Phineas Quimby**, who taught that the mind influences the body and environment long before science dared to explore such ideas. Then came **Emma Curtis Hopkins**, known as the "teacher of teachers," who trained the leaders of the New Thought movement and emphasized spiritual authority and the God-self within. **James Allen** showed the world that thought creates character and character creates destiny. **Wallace Wattles**, in *The Science of Getting Rich*, insisted that thinking in a "certain way" produces predictable results. **Florence Scovel Shinn** demonstrated the miraculous power of the spoken word, declaring that words are not mere sounds but commands issued to the universe.

And of course, **Napoleon Hill**, who spent two decades studying the most successful individuals of his time, concluded that the mind is the central architect of success. Every one of these teachers said the same thing in different ways:

You become what you repeatedly think, feel, and speak.

Even further back, ancient cultures held the same wisdom. The ancient Egyptians believed in *Heka*-the spiritual force activated through speech. The Hebrews understood the creative power of the tongue and the divine name *I Am That I Am* as the foundation of identity. The Stoics taught mastery of thought as the path to peace. Eastern traditions long emphasized the energy of intention and the vibration of mantra. Across continents and centuries, cultures who never met somehow shared the same truth: **Your internal world shapes your external one.**

Somehow, somewhere, this collective wisdom faded. We became so consumed with survival, productivity, and distraction that we forgot the spiritual mechanics that once guided humanity. But truth doesn't disappear — it simply waits for someone awake enough to retrieve it. One of my greatest passions is buying **vintage esoteric and early mind-science books** on eBay, the kind written in the 1600s, 1700s, and 1800s by mystics, philosophers, and metaphysical thinkers who understood the power of thought long before our modern language existed to describe it.

Somehow, somewhere, this collective wisdom faded. Humanity became so consumed with survival, productivity, deadlines, and distraction that we drifted away from the spiritual mechanics that once guided the inner life of our ancestors. But truth does not vanish—it simply waits for someone awake enough to retrieve it. And every time I hold one of my vintage books in my hands, I feel as though I'm reaching back through a doorway that the world forgot it had closed.

One of my greatest passions is collecting **vintage esoteric, mystical, and early mind-science books**, the kind you can only find through old bookstores or late-night eBay treasure hunts. My personal library includes works from brilliant early thinkers and metaphysical pioneers like **Philip K. Dick, Annie Besant, C. W. Leadbeater, Joseph Murphy, Henry M. Pachter, Orison Swett Marden, Robert Collier, William C. Schultz, Richard Gerber, Paul Brunton, and so many others** who understood long before us that the mind is a creative engine and consciousness is the architect of reality.

These were the teachers who carried forward the lineage of spiritual science, men and women who wrote about vibration before the word was popular, about imagination before psychology could explain it, about the Divine "**I Am**" before self-help existed as a genre.

Many of them were part of the early **Theosophical movement**, the **New Thought movement**, the **Transcendentalists**, and the revived **Hermetic and esoteric traditions** that bridged ancient spiritual principles with modern language. They were studying the same truths echoed in scripture, the same truths Jesus taught when He said, *"As a man thinketh in his heart, so is he."* Long before neuroscience proved that thought reshapes the brain, these thinkers boldly declared that thought reshapes destiny.

When I read their words, some written over a hundred years ago, I feel a sense of confirmation, as if the spiritual truths I've lived and learned were quietly understood by countless souls long before me. It comforts me to know that what I teach in these pages is not new at all. It is ancient, sacred, and timeless. It belongs to everyone.

And somehow, across centuries, it has found its way into my hands, into my heart, and now into this book.

And I cannot speak about this lineage of thought without honoring **Reverend Ike**, one of the boldest and most electrifying voices of the metaphysical movement, though he never called himself that. Reverend Ike was a bridge between traditional Christianity and spiritual mind science, a preacher who understood the Bible not just as a historical text, but as a **manual for personal transformation**.

I discovered him through old recordings on YouTube, and every time he spoke, I felt that same ancient truth rising to the surface: **your mind is the workshop of your life, and your words are the blueprints of your future.** He preached Jesus Christ and the power of God without apology, yet he also dared to say what many were too afraid to declare-that *poverty is not holy,* and that living a great life is not a sin. In fact, he taught that prosperity is a form of praise, because it honors the abundance of the God who created us.

Reverend Ike reminded his listeners that the "Kingdom of Heaven is within you," meaning your greatest source of power is not outside of you, waiting to be earned, but *inside you*, waiting to be used. He taught that **your imagination is your divine instrument**, your emotions are your spiritual fuel, and your "**I Am**" statements are the keys that unlock the life God already intended for you. His message was simple yet revolutionary:

You don't have to suffer to be spiritual. You don't have to be poor to be humble. You don't have to struggle to prove your faith.

Like the early metaphysical thinkers before him, Reverend Ike understood that consciousness creates experience. He spoke openly about the law of mind action, the power of belief, the creative word, and the sacred responsibility we each carry to shape our own lives. And yet, he never stepped away from Christ, he simply taught Christ's teachings from the inside out.

Reverend Ike's voice echoed the very principles I teach in this book: that God never intended for us to live small, broke, defeated, or spiritually starved. That our thoughts are prayers, our feelings are magnets, and our declarations are commands sent into the universe. When he said, *"You can't lose with the stuff I use,"* he was talking about **the mind aligned with divine identity.**

Listening to him affirmed what I already knew deep in my spirit: the message of "**I Am**" is not new, not trendy, and not metaphysical hype. It is the same eternal truth carried by mystics, prophets, metaphysicians, theologians, spiritual scientists, and everyday believers who dared to claim the power God placed within them.

Reverend Ike simply said it in a way that made people listen.

All of heir writings remind me that the "**I Am**" principle is not modern language, it is eternal language. It is the same divine declaration given to Moses at the burning bush. It is the same creative force spoken by mystics, shamans, sages, philosophers, and spiritual scientists across time. Whether they called it imagination, mind power, vibrational law, or divine identity, they were all pointing to the same truth:

*What you declare with "**I Am**," you become. What you believe in the invisible, you eventually witness in the visible. What you hold in consciousness, you hold in*
your reality.

This is why I treasure these books so deeply, they are a reminder that we are part of a long, unbroken lineage of souls awakening to the power of thought, the force of consciousness, and the holy resonance of the "**I Am.**"

And now, you are becoming part of that lineage too. And now, here you are, remembering it. This is why the content of this book feels familiar. Because on a soul level, you already know it. This is not learning; this is remembering who you originally are. This is not about adopting a new belief system; it is about reclaiming the one that was always yours.

The one your ancestors understood. The one ancient teachers preserved. The one mystics whispered. The one Jesus demonstrated. The one your spirit has been nudging you toward every time you instinctively said, *"I Am..."* without realizing the full power of those words.

When you understand the lineage of this truth, how far back it reaches, how deeply it runs, how consistently it has appeared across cultures, you begin to see that monitoring your thoughts is not merely positive thinking. It is sacred work. It is spiritual discipline. It is the modern expression of an ancient practice. And you realize that every time you choose a higher thought... every time you shift your vibration...every time you speak an "**I Am**" intentionally...you are standing in the same stream of wisdom that has guided enlightened souls for thousands of years.

I have four amazing children, one son and three daughters, and I absolutely adore them. One of the most powerful lessons I learned in maintaining positivity was understanding the importance of putting myself first. That may sound backward to some, especially to parents who were taught that self-sacrifice is the only measure of love. For years, I believed my feelings and needs did not matter as long as my children were happy.

That was the language I lived under. That was the agreement I silently made with life.

Now I understand differently. There is so much internal work required to live a happy, peaceful, emotionally balanced life. If you neglect yourself completely while pouring everything into others, you may wake up one day unfulfilled, depleted, and disconnected from your own joy. Life continues after parenthood. Children grow. They marry. They build their own worlds. And if you have not nurtured your own emotional and spiritual well-being, you can find yourself standing alone in silence, questioning who you are without the role you once played. Making sure your own mental and emotional needs are met is not selfish. It is necessary.

Because of my past, I grew up with many emotional deficiencies. I felt unwanted. My self-esteem was extremely low. I became a parent long before I ever attempted to heal my own wounds. Because I still carried so much unprocessed trauma, my love for my children became layered with fear. I was a great parent by society's standards. I worked hard. I provided everything they wanted and needed. I attended every school function. I showed affection. I encouraged them. I hugged and kissed them. I uplifted them. I was present. As far as I understood, I was doing everything right.

But I was neglecting myself completely. I did not even realize, in my early twenties and thirties, that I had unattended emotional needs. Although I knew I had experienced trauma, I did not know that healing was something I was allowed to seek. I did not know healing was even possible, let alone how to go about it. I did not recognize that many of my fears and reactions were directly connected to unresolved pain. I did not understand that the obsessive way in which I loved my children was rooted in fear of loss and abandonment rather than healthy attachment.

There are times when the behavior of children can be challenging. But when you are healed, you respond differently. When you are broken and needy, you excuse everything. You put them and others on a pedestal way above you, not realizing you too deserve to be there. You are also valuable and deserve the type of love you give to them. Once you begin to do your own inner work, you realize that you are just as worthy as anyone else, including your children. You deserve the same respect you give. You deserve the same boundaries you extend. Healing teaches you how to respond instead of react. Healing does not mean you will never feel hurt again. If means you will not react to it from your wombs. Best thing I have learned is to feel that feelings. Stop, take a breathe and process them as opposed to impulsively and instantly reacting out of hurt. Taking this advice will always give you a better outcome.

I remember a moment with my older sister that revealed how deeply my own unhealed wounds were influencing my perception. When she was away at college, she once told me she would not be coming home for Thanksgiving. Today, that sounds like a normal decision for a young student adjusting to adult life. But at that time, my reaction was devastation. I cried. I internalized it. I took it personally. I believed her choice meant I was not important enough to come home to see. In truth, her decision had nothing to do with me. She was building her life. But because I had not healed my own abandonment wounds from childhood, I interpreted her independence as rejection. That is what unresolved pain does. It teaches you to suffer unnecessarily. Suffering is a choice we do not have to make.

If I had not begun healing, I would have been emotionally destroyed when my children grew up and began moving away from home. Most parents expect and celebrate that independence. But when abandonment issues live within you, separation feels like betrayal. When my oldest daughter left for college, she slipped away while I was at work because she knew a long, emotional goodbye would overwhelm both of us. Years earlier, I would have interpreted that as cruelty. But because I was healing, I understood. My perspective had matured. My language had changed. My identity had shifted. You must seek healing and begin to view yourself as a priority or simply events , like kids going off to college will destroy you. Start with the simple "**I Am**" affirmations:

I Am Loved, **I Am** Valuable, **I Am** Happy, **I Am** Content, **I Am** Peaceful, **I Am** Enough

Even if these affirmations do not register as truth yet, keep saying them until they do. There is no specific time frame to complete this healing work. Re-programming self sabotaging beliefs is the ultimate goal, so it may take a while to shift beliefs you have been cultivating for many years. However it is possible. Please do not give up.

When healing begins, your entire perspective widens. You stop viewing everything as a personal attack. You start to develop the strength to pause, breathe, and consider the feelings and intentions of others without filtering every moment through old wounds. And little by little, something shifts. I kept doing the work. I kept choosing myself. And today, at 56, many of the emotional "holes" I once carried have finally closed. I know now that I am worthy of love and happiness, not because of how my life began, but because of who I am. And **so are you**.

I no longer need validation from anyone. I am confident in the woman I've become and deeply proud of the life I've built. I raised four children alone. I ran a successful business for over 30 years. I stood on more than sixty stages, sharing my story and uplifting thousands. And now, in this new season of my life, I plan to spend the second half writing books that help people transform their lives from the inside out.

No more depression. No more suffering. No more playing small. I pray my books heal hearts, inspire success, and remind people that they are extraordinary beings, powerful beyond measure, and that the story of their past does **not** define the brilliance of their future.

But that healing did not fall from the sky. I had to pursue it. I had to seek it diligently. I had to stop calling myself broken and scarred. I had to stop viewing the world as the enemy. I had to stop being angry with God. I had to forgive myself and others. I had to change my language about my past, my parents, and myself and making those decisions changed my life.

The most powerful shift came when I learned to gain control over my own thoughts. From a book called "The Untethered Soul" by Michael Singer. It taught me about the importance of monitoring my thoughts. I practiced replacing negative thoughts with positive ones over and over until it became habitual.

That is what I want for each of you. Switching out negative language for life-giving language must become second nature. Your mind is the tool that transforms your earthly experience. What you speak is the program you run through that tool. What you speak from your mouth shapes your entire life.

You do not speak to impress the world. You speak to align yourself with who God made you to be. You speak to agree with who you are becoming rather than who you used to be. You speak to remind your soul of truth when your environment tries to teach you something lower. Every "I can," every "I have", every "**I Am**" releases motion into your future. Positive motion that shapes your reality.

The universe responds to consistency before it responds to volume. It is easy to speak power when life is going well. The real discipline of words is revealed under pressure. What you say when you are tired, disappointed, overlooked, and hurt tells you exactly who is leading your life in that moment, faith or impulsive reaction.

Your words are either building the bridge you will one day walk across or dismantling the very path you're praying to travel. Intentional speech isn't about being perfect, it's about being aware. The more conscious you become of the language you release into the world, the more authority you reclaim over your destiny. As *Invictus* reminds us, **"You become the master of your fate."**

When you speak, you are not only shaping circumstances. You are shaping your nervous system, your emotions, your confidence, and your spiritual posture. You are teaching your body how to respond to life. You are teaching your spirit what to expect next. Your words prepare you for either expansion or retreat.

You were never meant to be a silent witness to your own life. You were created to participate in it, to speak into it, to call things forward long before you ever hold them in your hands. You were designed to align with Heaven even in the moments when earth feels uncertain. The power isn't in pretending; the power is in agreeing with truth even while that truth is still unfolding.

Scripture teaches us this clearly: *"Faith is the substance of things hoped for, the evidence of things not seen"* (Hebrews 11:1). And Romans 4:17 affirms that God *"calls things that are not as though they were."*

When you speak in alignment with that truth, you are not making things up, you are partnering with what already exists in the spirit until it shows up in the natural.

Let today be the last day you speak **Lack & Limitation**, **Death & Doom**, **Sickness & Poverty** over your own life. Let today be the last day you use phrases like "I Can't". Today you realize your voice is not small. Your words will not be random. Your declarations and affirmations are not invisible. You have been planting, watering, healing, and shaping with every sentence you have ever spoken. Now you get to choose to do it on purpose. **Your future is listening so watch your words.**

The reason I am so passionate about teaching you these concepts is because I used to be poor. Not financially but spiritually. I was poor in faith, poor in belief, poor in identity. I had a low self-esteem and a poverty mindset. I was emotionally depleted because of my past trauma. I now know that God did not intend for us to suffer or struggle mentally, spiritually, emotionally, or financially. But back then, I had no idea of my greatness. I figure if my own mother did not want and love me then who would. But we were all created from love, and this universe we live in is abundant. It is ready and waiting to bestow that abundance upon us. No matter what you have experienced in your life, you are a magnificent creation of God. Do not allow anyone-even yourself to tell you differently.

We are supposed to experience wealth in all areas: mental,

physical, spiritual, emotional, and financial. But abundance cannot stay where the mind rejects it. You must become rich mentally and emotionally before you can attain financial abundance. Otherwise, you won't be able to sustain it because you won't believe you deserve it.

Once we fall in love with ourselves, once we stop tormenting ourselves with past events, once we accept that we deserve the best that life has to offer, our finances follow suit. Spiritual richness must take precedence. Become rich internally first.

Most of our parents and grandparents had a poverty mindset. They believed lack was destiny. They believed disease was inherited and unavoidable. They believed wealth was sinful or greedy. They believed that hard work should only produce "just enough" to get by. They were beautiful people. They simply did not know any better.

Generational limitations are simply unchallenged beliefs passed down. Mental poverty is inherited long before financial poverty is. But now we know differently. And because we know differently, we can choose differently. I believe it's part of the systematic evolution of mankind. I believe it was designed for us to wake up to our greatness eventually. We must individually seek that evolution though. It is not a given that you will evolve. Many people made it to the graveyard and never understood the power and control they had over their own lives.

We can indeed change our thought patterns. We can break the cycle.

We can rewire the inner dialogue. We can rewrite our **I AM's.**

Once we understand the creative power of our thoughts, we should teach our children and their children to embrace prosperity, happiness, love, health, and abundance without guilt or hesitation. We can have it all. We don't have to sacrifice joy to be spiritual. We don't have to abandon wealth to be close to God. The Divine Source that created us-is for us, not against us. God is not your enemy, your negative internal dialog is.

Learning a more positive way of thinking changed my entire life. It unlocked the God-given power within me, a power we all possess. It is limitless, timeless, and abundant.

I want everyone who reads this chapter to tap into their own power. Once you acquire this knowledge and use it, you become fearless. You become invincible. You realize that all things are possible and that there is absolutely nothing you cannot do.

The only limitations that truly exist are the ones we accept in our minds. We live in a time where knowledge is accessible, tools are abundant, and the spiritual veil is thinner than ever. Our ancestors prayed we would understand these truths. Now it is our responsibility to apply them, embody them, and pass them forward.

We must show our children their power by living in ours.

We must demonstrate abundance by walking in abundance.

We must model faith by speaking faith.

We must teach confidence by declaring, daily:

"**I AM** capable. **I AM** strong. **I AM** worthy. **I AM** focused. **I AM** prepared. **I AM** already everything God created me to be." I simply have to remember and start walking bravely in that greatness.

Mental poverty leads to poverty in every other area of life. But the moment you shift your I AM, your entire world begins to transform.

Free your mind - and you will follow.

I love my children. They have been the driving force behind my desire to live a more fulfilling life. I wanted to ensure they never felt abandoned, hurt, or unwanted. I worked hard for over 30 years as a small business owner to take care of them financially. That part was easy. The challenge was facing myself.

I adored and wanted all of my babies, but deep inside, I was afraid, afraid they would get hurt by life as I had, afraid they would grow up and leave me behind, afraid life would take them from me the way other people had been taken from me. I was loving through fear. And fear is not love. Fear is attachment masquerading as love.

A friend once told me something that changed my life:

"Our children are gifts from God, but they are not ours."

We are simply the portal they come through. They are here to live their own lives, walk their own journeys, and discover their own paths. Understanding that truth loosened my grip and increased my trust.

Healing allowed me to love without fear.

Healing allowed me to give them room to grow.

Healing allowed my **I AM** to shift from "I am afraid" to "I am trusting."

And as I healed, my children began to meet the real me, the whole me, the woman underneath the wounds.

Being their mother has been one of the greatest honors of my life. They were band-aids at first, covering wounds I didn't yet know how to treat. But each time they grew older and no longer needed me the same way, those band-aids peeled back, revealing pain I had ignored. And eventually, I realized my babies were never meant to heal me. That was my work to do. That was my journey. Many of you readers are also on a journey of healing. I lived long enough and cam in contact with enough people to realize, there are a lot of hurt people in this world.

It wasn't until I became a motivational speaker that my children ever heard my full story. I had shielded them from the darkness, believing it was too heavy for their innocence. And when they asked about my mother, I found creative ways to answer, gentle ways, until I was finally ready to unveil the truth.

I attended Centennial High School in Compton, CA. Whenever someone at school asked about my biological mother, I would tell them she had died. That wasn't true. My mother was a drug addict who abandoned me and my older sister when we were just babies-eleven months and three months old. We were born so close in age that most people thought we were twins. My sister Mary was born August 24, 1968, and I was born August 7, 1969. Our mother didn't raise either of us. But before she left our lives fully, she put me into a suitcase at three months old and attempted to take my life.

My amazing grandmother, Ella Mae Fisher Fair, rescued and raised me alongside my sister, until we lost her in the most tragic way imaginable. After thirty-two years of marriage, her husband, our grandfather, McClendon Fair, took her life in front of me with a single gunshot wound to the head. I was seventeen years old and a senior in high school. My life changed forever that day.

I suffered for years with depression and PTSD. By the time I reached my forties, I was desperate to heal. I had already begun the journey, but I didn't yet have the tools I have now. So I ran toward church, because it was all I knew. It was the only lifeline I had. I grew up in Ephesians Church of God in Christ in Compton, California. My grandmother was a member of the Mothers' Board. Every Sunday she stood before the congregation and sang:

> *The fight is on, the trumpet sound is ringing out,*
> *The cry "To arms!" is heard afar and near;*
> *The Lord of hosts is marching on to victory............*

It is Amazing to me I still remember that song and I am fifty-six years old.

My grandmothers faith held me until my own faith could stand on its own. Her prayers covered me and my sister-even from her grave. And when I eventually walked into the darkest emotional season of my life, I ran back to the only place I knew offered comfort: the church. I hopped from church to church, searching for a healing I would later discover had to begin within me. The truth is, no human being can heal you. People can guide, support, and inspire, but the real work—the awakening, the releasing, the rebuilding—comes from the power already living inside you.

Along that journey, as the layers of pain slowly lifted, I began to develop positive tools that helped me sustain every level of healing I reached. Those tools became my survival kit, my compass, my inner foundation. And it is my prayer that this book becomes that tool for someone else. If even one person feels lighter, stronger, more hopeful, or more connected to their own healing because of these words, then my work is complete. I am fulfilling my purpose—and that brings me joy.

Healing starts within. Suffering is a choice we do not have to keep making. Freedom begins with a new **I AM**.

THE MIRACLE OF "**I AM**

This is why the "**I AM**" statement is the most powerful

spiritual command you possess. Every time you say "**I AM**," you are not describing yourself. You are instructing your future. You are activating spiritual law. You are telling your mind what to build. You are telling your nervous system what to expect. You are telling God what you are ready to align with. "**I AM**" is not passive language. It is creation. It is identity. It is permission. It is prophecy.

When you say:

I AM worthy — you call worthiness toward you. **I AM healing** — your body begins to shift. **I AM wealthy** — prosperity and abundance flow towards you. **I AM powerful** — your energy rises to meet that truth.

Everything transforms at the level of **I AM.** So let this chapter serve as your turning point. Let this serve as the tool you always needed to get you on the right track towards building the future you desire.

You are not your wounds. You are not your mistakes. You are not someone elses mistakes. You are not your fears. You are not your struggles. You are the powerful "**I AM**" that you choose to speak Now! Say it with conviction. Say it with passion. Say it with authority.

"**I Am That I Am**" **I AM** ready. **I AM** enough. **I AM** successful. **I AM** aligned. **I AM** blessed. **I AM** chosen. **I AM** loved. **I AM** powerful. **I AM** expanding. **I AM** free. And watch — truly watch — how your entire life rises to meet those words.

5

Identity Creates Reality

How who you believe yourself to be shapes everything you experience.

Identity is the invisible architect of your life. Long before a circumstance ever appears, it is first shaped by who you believe yourself to be. You do not rise to the level of your dreams, you live at the level of your perceived identity. Your habits, your choices, your boundaries, your relationships, and even your prayers are all filtered through the picture you hold of yourself within.

You do not chase what you think is beyond you. You reach naturally for what you believe you deserve. This is why two people can receive the same opportunity and experience completely different outcomes. One sees it as a miracle they cannot lose. The other sees it as something they were never meant to keep. Identity controls expectancy, and expectancy controls behavior.

Many people try to change their lives without ever changing

how they see themselves. They set goals with an old self-image. They ask for abundance while still identifying as someone who struggles. They constantly yell phrases like: "I'm broke" and wonder why its a reality. They pray for elevation while still speaking the language of limitation. And then they feel confused when their results do not match their requests. But the truth is simple: your life will always move in agreement with your strongest self-definition. So take some time and sit alone with yourself and figure out what you truly believe about you. I' not speaking about the fluffed up Bio that we all have in Google Docs ready to print. Who are you sincerely? The authentic you.

What you consistently say about yourself becomes the blueprint for your future. When you identify as strong, you endure differently. When you identify as worthy, you receive differently. When you identify as chosen, you walk with quiet confidence even before evidence arrives. Identity does not wait for proof. It becomes proof through consistency.

Trauma, disappointment, rejection, and hurt all try to rewrite your identity if you allow them to speak louder than truth. Life may introduce you to pain, but only *you* decide whether pain becomes your name. You can experience loss without identifying as lost. You can experience struggle without identifying as broken. You can walk through fire without accepting the identity of ashes.

That was a lesson I am so grateful I finally learned. For a long time, I identified as a victim because of everything I had endured. And honestly, it made sense. It fit. It applied. One day, during a seminar, I referred to myself as a survivor, and the facilitators of the event nearly hit the ceiling. They got right in my face and said, "This better be the last time you call yourself a survivor." Then they asked me, "Is that all you want to do in

46

this life... survive?"

I was stunned. Horrified. Confused. I didn't understand why they reacted so strongly. Later, they explained: "You do not just want to survive in this life. You want to **thrive**."

That seminar cost me $2,000, and it was the best $2,000 I ever spent. As intense as it was, it cracked something open in me. It expanded my mind. And from that day forward, I have never again referred to myself as a survivor. I made a decision to identify with my future, not my wounds.

"What has happened to you, is not you."

You identity is not what has happened to you. Identity is what you decide to become after what happened to you. And this decision is reinforced daily through language, belief, and the quiet expectations you hold when no one is watching. You live as the version of yourself that you agree with most.

The most powerful shift happens when identity moves from reaction to intention. When you stop waiting for life to confirm who you are, and you start declaring who you want to be. When your words, actions, and self-talk begin to reflect the future you desire rather than the history you survived. Then you are embarking upon a life-changing mindset shift.

You are not waiting for life to change so you can believe differently. Life is waiting for you to believe differently so it can change. Read that Again!

Here are a few identity-anchoring affirmations to align your inner image with your highest reality:

I am capable of being the highest version of who I was created to be.

47

I **am** worthy of growth, love, peace, and abundance.
I **am** no longer defined by my past, but by my purpose.
I **am** aligned with opportunity, clarity, and divine direction.
I **am** walking in confidence, even while I am still unfolding.

Now it is time for you to create your own. Your affirmations should be spoken in the present tense, emotionally charged with belief, and connected to the identity you are calling forth. Use the lines below to begin shaping your personal declarations of truth:

Speak only what you desire to become, not what you fear.
   Write in the present tense, as if the change is already happen-ing.
   Avoid negative language or references to lack.
   Focus on identity before circumstance.
   Read each affirmation aloud at least once a day.
   Return to these lines when fear tries to rename you.
   Update your affirmations as your confidence grows.
   Let emotion strengthen the truth you are speaking.
   Remember that repetition is the bridge between belief and embodiment.
   Identity creates reality. What you agree with about yourself today is quietly shaping the life you will walk into tomorrow.

Write your own personalized "**I AM**" statements:

————————————————————————————

————————————————————————————

Say these with confidence to yourself in the mirror daily.

The moment you change what you call yourself, you begin to change what your life must answer to. Your destiny is not waiting on permission from the world, it is waiting on agreement from your own mouth. When you speak your true identity with confidence and faith, your future can no longer deny you.

6

Becoming What You Speak

The transformation that happens when your words and actions align.

Every word you speak is a rehearsal for who you are becoming. Long before you ever walk in it, you practice it with your mouth. Long before it ever manifests in form, it manifests in faith through language. Long before you lived the reality of it, you visualized it in your mind. You are always moving in the direction of your dominant declarations, whether you recognize it or not. What you repeatedly speak is what you eventually live.

At first, your words may feel imaginary. It may feel like you are playing a childhood pretend game. But this is the ultimate key to bringing it forth. You can speak strength while still feeling weak. You can speak abundance while still facing lack. You must speak confidence even while still wrestling with insecurity. Initially it may feel like you are lying to yourself. Don't stop.

I have a chapter in one of my earlier books called **"Fake It**

Until You Feel It." The mouth speaks the future long before the body catches up. This is the sacred space where transformation is born — the place where what you say does not yet fully match what you see. But if you continue using these daily manifestation tools, that gap will close, and your words will soon become your reality.

Words are energy, and it has been my experience that repeatedly saying an affirmation aloud will eventually invoke the feeling — and the feeling is the last puzzle piece. Just try it; you have absolutely nothing to lose. Once we couple the positive words with the emotion of already having what we desire, that is when the magic of manifestation happens. The consistent speaking of the words *plus* the feeling of possession is the perfect recipe for creating a great life for yourself.

Many unfortunate situations can and will happen in life. When we allow ourselves to feel bad, we lower our energetic vibration. Even when we are justified in reacting negatively, we still cannot allow ourselves to stay in that negative state of mind. Thinking negatively lowers our vibration, and when we are vibrating at a low frequency, we attract all things that match that same low level. That is why it is vital to learn to raise our vibration as soon as we wake up in the morning. We must elevate our energy before we step outside, or the world will decide our vibration for us.

Do not be discouraged when you have been praying and doing your affirmations and it still seems things aren't moving fast enough for you. Don't get upset with God and think He has failed you. Growth is not instant, but it is always intentional. The seed spoken today does not stand tall tomorrow, yet it is already alive beneath the surface. In the same way, every affirmation you make is quietly shaping the parts of you that are still developing.

You are not lying when you speak your future — you are teaching yourself how to become it.

Becoming the best version of yourself requires consistency. One positive statement spoken in frustration will not erase years of negative self-talk. But one clear affirmation spoken repeatedly will eventually rewrite the story your subconscious has been telling your life. Do not grow impatient with the process. You are undoing habits of identity that may have taken decades to form. Be patient with yourself, but stay consistent.

Your words begin as clearly defined intention, then they become belief, then they become behavior, and finally they become your biography. This is why change feels awkward at first. You are speaking from a future identity while still standing in a former version of yourself. But this is how all elevation begins—by daring to sound like who you want to become even while you are still becoming.

You will not always feel aligned with what you speak. Feelings fluctuate. Declarations will help to establish direction. Feelings follow what you give authority to over time. If you wait to feel powerful before you speak power, you will remain silent far too long. You speak first. You align later. You become last. It does not matter who you are now or who you used to be. You can become a different person if you choose to.

What you speak repeatedly becomes familiar. What becomes familiar begins to feel possible. What feels possible eventually becomes natural. And what becomes natural becomes your lifestyle. This is the quiet, subtle progression of becoming. No fireworks. No instant magic. Just steady agreement between your mouth, your mind, and your future.

Be careful not to sabotage who you are becoming by returning to old language out of comfort. Familiar pain can feel safer than unfamiliar promise. Sometimes the greatest battle is not between good and evil, but between the person you have been and the person you are courageously allowing yourself to become. Your mouth will reveal which one is currently leading.

If you slip up and say something self-defeating, be thankful, it means you're finally aware of it. Awareness is growth. Simply acknowledge it, correct it, and speak something better. What's that old saying? *"One positive thought has more power than many negative thoughts."*

So go easy on yourself and start again. Eventually, uplifting yourself and speaking about yourself in a positive manner will become a habit, a natural part of your new identity.

You are not becoming what others label you as. You are becoming what you consistently agree with about yourself. The world may try to define you by your past, your mistakes, your season of struggle, or your waiting period. But your words have authority over those labels when they are spoken in faith and repeated with conviction.

Becoming is not passive. It is participatory. You speak, then you act. You declare, then you align. You believe, then you walk. Your mouth opens the door. Your obedience walks you through it. And your consistency builds the life you prayed for.

There will be days when you feel like nothing is changing. Speak anyway. There will be days when doubt feels louder than truth. Speak anyway. There will be days when you feel unqualified to declare anything powerful about yourself. Speak anyway. Your future is not built on how you feel in the moment. It is built on what you choose to speak in spite of how you feel. So do not abandon your "**I AM**" statements when you are feeling bad. Those are the times when you need them.

When you say "**I AM**" you are not just talking. You are training your life. You are teaching your spirit what to expect. You are instructing your subconscious what to pursue. You are shaping your nervous system to recognize the identity you are stepping into. Every declaration is a brick. Every repetition is another layer in the foundation of who you are becoming.

You do not become accidentally. You become intentionally. And your words are the blueprint. You are not who you used to be. You are not even who you feel like today. You are who you keep speaking yourself into.

And your future is listening.

7

The Internal You

Discovering the unseen world within that governs the world around you.

Whether or not we have come to accept it, we are advanced vibrational beings. Just like dormant cells in our bodies, there is no guarantee that we will individually operate at an advanced level. We were placed on this earth to do far more than eat, sleep, work, and repeat day after day. Each one of us carries a personal purpose and a significant gift meant to be released into this world. As strongly as I believe that we are all here for a specific purpose, I also believe that there is no guarantee that we will discover that purpose before we die. There are many people buried in the graveyard that never reached their highest potential. that does not have to be you.

There are signs and clues released throughout our lives that quietly point us toward our destiny, but most of us are too busy, too distracted, or too conditioned by routine to recognize them. I believe these signs often show up as sudden bursts of inspiration or as recurring thoughts, ideas, and dreams that refuse to leave us alone. When these moments arrive, they are not random. They are invitations. It is the presence of Divine energy. And when it arrives, we must take advantage of those moment. Do not let those moments pass.

I suggest taking immediate action by writing down everything that comes to your mind. Do not depend on memory, because from my own experience, memory can and will fail you. There is no guarantee that those same ideas will return in the same clarity again. When great ideas suddenly pop into my mind, I call it my "Inspiration for Creation", a natural, divine ability given to us by God to create, expand, and design a magnificent life. If you ever feel a sudden, compelling urge to do something, especially something you have never considered before, listen to it, give in to it. I believe that is the divine spirit gently but firmly pushing you toward your true destiny.

We read books and watch documentaries about great inventors, visionaries, and leaders who have changed the world with their creations. We admire them, study them, and celebrate them. But what we often forget is this: the very same divine energy that empowered them to create great things is very much alive and present inside of each of us. There is greatness within you. Every person has the ability to create-whether it is in their personal life or through ideas meant to advance humanity as a whole.

Although this creative power exists in all of us, many people never activate it. They accept limitations handed to them by fear, trauma, environment, or tradition. Some can't tune into the powerful energy because they numb themselves with drugs and alcohol. They shrink their expectations to match their surroundings. Over time, they forget what they once felt stirring inside of them. They give up on ideas and settle for mediocrity in their lives. It is up to each of us individually to activate this power from within. I believe the world cannot fully advance collectively until each person chooses to advance individually. We all have that unlimited power of God within us, but it is up to us to use it.

The first step is identifying the mental and emotional barriers we have built that prevent us from living a productive, purpose-filled life. These barriers are often invisible to others but loud to our spirit. They speak as doubt. They speak as delay. They speak as self-sabotage. They speak as fear of being seen, fear of failure, and sometimes even fear of success. Yet behind all of these lies the internal you—the true you—waiting patiently to be acknowledged and activated.

My belief in this is not rooted in scientific data but in personal observation throughout my life. I have watched countless people live and die operating only at an ordinary level, not because they lacked potential, but because they never believed they were allowed to be extraordinary. Yet I have also witnessed a few who dared to believe what was speaking inside of them—and their lives expanded accordingly. The difference was never intellect. It was always belief and confidence.

Stop acting ordinary when God clearly created you to be an extraordinary being.

The internal you is powerful. It is intuitive. It is creative. It is emotionally intelligent. It is spiritually alive. It is aware of more than you consciously allow yourself to acknowledge. Before logic arrives, the internal you already knows. Before opportunity manifests, the internal you already senses it. This is why certain ideas will not leave you alone. This is why some dreams return year after year even when you try to ignore them. This is why your spirit becomes restless when you have stayed in one place too long. God has given us free will and control over our own lives. I have witness personally, times when God will nudge you down your ideal path. It may be subtle, it may come through signs and symbols. The key is being still long enough to recognize Gods help.

Your internal world is always communicating with your outer world. The life you desire externally is already being shaped internally through imagination, intention, and belief. Before a thing ever exists in your hands, it must exist in your awareness. The unseen always precedes the seen.

Many people wait for permission to become who they already are inside. They wait for validation. They wait for perfect conditions. They wait for someone else to agree with them. But the internal you does not need permission. It needs acceptance and agreement. When you agree with what is stirring within you, doors begin to open that logic alone could never unlock.

Inside of you are ideas that could create legacy. Inside of you are solutions to problems you may not yet see. Inside of you are businesses that have not yet been built, books that have not yet been written, inventions that have not yet been designed, and ministries that have not yet been activated. Your imagination is a gift. Use it to start designing the new blueprint of your life.

The tragedy is not that people fail. The tragedy is that many people never try. They silence the internal voice with hectic daily routine. They quiet destiny with distraction. They suppress calling with comfort. And over time, what once felt loud becomes faint. Yet even then, it never fully disappears.

The internal you is patient. But it is persistent.

Now is the time to pause and listen again. Be still, take a deep breath and envision how you want to next chapter of your life to unfold.

Use the lines below to list some amazing ideas or sudden bursts of inspiration you have experienced in your life. These may be inventions, business ideas, upgrades to existing systems, creative projects, or improvements meant to serve others. Write without censoring yourself.

1.

2.

3.

4.

5.

6.

Periodically return to these ideas. Speak them aloud. Pray over them. Then begin to assign a real, practical plan to bring each one into fruition. Do not wait for perfection. Progress responds to movement, not to hesitation.

Your destiny is not outside of you. It is within you. The internal you already knows the way. Your only responsibility is to finally listen—and then make it happen.

8

I Am That I Am

Stepping fully into divine identity, authority, and spiritual alignment.

"I Am That I Am." These words echo through time, spirit, and identity. They are not only the declaration of the Divine—they are an invitation for you to understand who you truly are. When you say "**I Am,**" you are not just describing yourself. You are aligning yourself with the most powerful creative force in existence. You are stepping into agreement with life, purpose, and divine design.

From the moment you were born, life began trying to label you. Some labels were helpful. Many were limiting. Some were spoken in love. Others were spoken in fear, pain, or misunderstanding. Over time, those labels tried to become your identity. But your true identity was never meant to be defined by circumstance, failure, success, age, background, or opinion. Your true identity begins with "**I Am.**"

Every season of life responds to the name you call yourself. Children become what they are told they are. Adults often live under the weight of what they once believed about themselves. Seniors sometimes forget the power that still lives within them. But at any age, in any season, at any moment, the power of "**I Am**" can rewrite the story instantly.

"I am strong."
   "I am loved."
   "I am capable."
   "I am chosen."
   "I am enough."
Each of these is more than encouragement. They are commands to the soul.

When God spoke to Moses through the burning bush and declared, **"I Am That I Am"** (Exodus 3:14), He wasn't just identifying Himself — He was establishing the foundation of all creation, all identity, and all spiritual law. "**I Am**" is the name of God. "**I Am**" is the nature of God. And "**I Am**" is the power of God placed inside you.

When you say "**I Am**," you are not simply describing yourself — you are aligning with the most creative force in the universe. You are agreeing with divine truth or denying it. You are building or breaking your future with the words you attach to God's name. Remember you negative "I Am's" hold equal power. That is why it is vital that you "I Am"statements are positive. If you say "I Am dumb", "I Am broke", "I Am sick," then that is what you will call forth.

There comes a moment in every spiritual journey when you realize that God never asked you to shrink, to dim your light, or to wait for permission to become who you were created to be. Somewhere along the way, religion, fear, or the opinions of wounded people convinced us that humility meant hiding, or that holiness meant pretending we were less than divine creation. But that was never God's intention. From the very beginning, God introduced Himself with a name that wasn't small, timid, or insecure. He said, **"I Am That I Am."** That statement was pure identity, pure authority, pure truth.

And whether you realize it or not, you were made in the image of that same God. When you say **"I Am,"** you are not making a cute, trendy statement or speaking empty words, you are stepping into agreement with the identity God placed inside you before your first breath. From infancy, the world tried to name you. Parents, teachers, lovers, enemies, society, mistakes, trauma — they all tried to label you. Some labels were loving. Others were cruel. None of them had the right to define you. Your true name has always begun where God's name begins: **with I Am.**

Life responds to whatever follows those words. Children grow into the names they hear. Adults carry the weight of names spoken over them years ago. Elders forget the power still living in their spirit because no one reminds them. But identity is never lost, it is only forgotten. This knowledge has always been there, lost or burned in ancient books. Buried with many of our ancient philosophers. But mankind is evolving and remembering. I'm grateful top be alive during this time.

The moment you reclaim **"I Am,"** the moment you dare to speak yourself into alignment again, something shifts in the unseen. You can feel it. When you declare **"I Am That I Am"** doors begin to open. When you whisper "I am rising," strength returns to your bones. When you remember "I am created in

God's image," shame loses its authority.

The truth is, you were never waiting on the world to validate you — the world was waiting on you to agree with God. The same divine breath that declared "**I Am That I Am**" is the breath living inside your words today. You carry creative power because you were formed by a Creative Source. You carry spiritual authority because you were shaped by a God who speaks realities into being. You carry infinite possibility because the One who formed you designed you without limits.

And yet, somewhere between childhood innocence and adult responsibility, we learned to doubt our own power. We learned to accept the labels and the limitations handed to us. We learned to call ourselves names God never wrote in our spirit. We learned to shrink so others could feel comfortable. We learned to deny the greatness God placed inside us out of fear that someone might misunderstand or call us arrogant.

But you were never meant to live at the level of other people's understanding. You were meant to live at the level of God's intention. And God's intention has always been abundance, expansion, growth, purpose, love, creativity, prosperity, healing, clarity, and truth. God never said, "You are weak." He said, "Let the weak say **I Am strong**." God never said, "You are stuck." He said, "Be transformed by the renewing of your mind." God never said, "You are hopeless." He said, "With Me, **all things are possible**."

When you connect these truths, when you realize that the same God who said "I Am That I Am" breathed His nature into you, the phrase **"When I say I Am..."** becomes a spiritual key to open the doors of the life you were meant to lead. It becomes the doorway between who you have been and who you are becoming. It becomes the bridge between struggle and possibility, between fear and faith, between the life you see and the life you are calling forward.

Every shift begins in your identity and every manifestation begins in your mouth. In the great power of you tongue. Every transformation begins in the beliefs you allow to anchor in your subconscious mind. And when you begin to understand the weight of those two words — *I Am* — you begin to understand yourself, your power, and your God on a completely different level.

When life gets heavy, it becomes easy to forget this power. A denied home loan, a relationship slipping through your fingers, a job loss, a repossessed car, a phone call that breaks your spirit — these are the moments when "I Am" feels the hardest to believe. These are the moments when fear whispers louder than faith, when circumstances attempt to rename you, when doubt tries to convince you that God has forgotten your name.

But if "I Am That I Am" means anything, it means this:

God is not defined by circumstances, and neither are you.

Your circumstances may shift, your emotions may waver, but your identity remains untouched. You were created with spiritual authority, and that authority does not disappear because life grows uncomfortable. When the world shakes, you are not meant to crumble, you are meant to remember who you are.

Remember that you are energy.

Remember that your spirit vibrates.

Remember that everything in existence — from your cells to your thoughts — is alive and moving. They are vibrating at a frequency that you now know you can control.

We look solid, but we are not. We are frequency held together by intention. We are all vibrational beings. We are consciousness wrapped in skin. We are spirit expressing itself through form. And the beautiful truth is this: **your vibration is not fixed**. You can raise it. You can shift it. You can breathe and speak yourself into a higher frequency the same way your words caused you to operate at a lower vibration. It is all in your hands.

That is why the Bible says, *"Be transformed by the renewing of your mind."* Transformation begins internally. Identity shifts internally. Breakthrough begins internally. Even Jesus said, *"As you believe, so shall it be done unto you."* Not as you wish. Not as you fear. As you believe.

Belief lives in the subconscious mind, the deep, silent place where your real identity is stored. When what you say with your mouth finally matches what you believe in that deeper place, you come into alignment. And alignment is where miracles happen.

You are not powerless in your own life. You are not a victim of your emotions. You are not at the mercy of whatever mood you wake up in. Once I realized I could change the way I felt, everything changed for me. I no longer had to accept a bad mood as my destiny for the day. I learned that if I caught my emotions early enough, I could redirect them — through gospel music, through 432hz frequencies, through gratitude, through silent meditation, through breath. I began to understand that I didn't have to let the morning dictate the whole day. I could shift my vibration at any moment. We all have that same control over how we want to begin our day. And when I started shifting my vibration, my life started shifting too.

Not because God suddenly started blessing me more, but because I moved into alignment with the blessings that were already mine. God never withholds or punishes like some believe. We simply learn, over time, through trial and prayer, how to rise into agreement with what God already said is possible.

"All things are possible" is not a metaphor. It is a spiritual law. Just like gravity. Just like sowing and reaping. Just like the vibration of your thoughts returning to you multiplied. Low energy attracts more low energy and high energy attracts more high energy. Fear attracts what fear focuses on and faith attracts what faith calls forward.

This is why you cannot afford to let your negative thoughts run wild. Not because God is punishing you, but because **your thoughts have creative authority.** They plant seeds in the subconscious soil. They form the blueprint your life builds itself around. They whisper instructions to your vibration. And the level you choose to vibrate on is what you will experience.

Identity determines frequency, and frequency determines manifestation.

"**I Am**" is not a phrase. It a command. It is a tuning fork. It pulls your life into harmony with the truth you choose to believe.

At some point on this journey, you must decide who you are going to believe, your fear or your faith, your past history or your spirit, your current circumstances or your Creator. There comes a moment when repeating old language no longer feels comfortable, when shrinking no longer fits, when settling becomes too painful to tolerate, and when your soul quietly whispers, *"Remember who you are."*

That whisper is God.

The same God who stood before Moses and said, **"I Am That I**

Am."

The same God who breathed identity into existence.

The same God who embedded creative power into every human spirit.

The same God who placed His likeness within you so you could co-author your life with Him. And understand I say Him for communications sake alone. Him, He is what humans are used to, but there is no way that the amazing ,divine, omnipotent, unseen energy that I choose to call God is a man alone. God is All! that includes male and female energy. But that's a subject for another book lol.

When God revealed Himself as *I Am,* it was not for His benefit. It was to show you the blueprint of identity. Every time you say **"I Am..."** you are not only describing yourself, you are proclaiming your Divine inheritance. You are activating spiritual law. You are calling forward the version of yourself that already exists in God's mind. You are choosing which frequency your life will respond to.

This is why your words matter.

This is why your thoughts matter.

This is why your vibration matters.

You are not here to beg life for scraps. You are here to **name** your reality and walk in agreement with that name. The universe is not confused. It responds to whatever identity you embody most consistently.

If you say "I am tired," life will give you reasons to stay tired.

If you say "I am unlucky," life will mirror that belief.

If you say "I am unworthy," your blessings will wait at the

door until you open it from the inside. But the moment you say:

"I AM Worthy."

"I AM Capable."

"I Am Happy"

"I Am Successful"

"I AM Prosperous."

"I AM becoming the fullest expression of God within me," your entire spiritual climate shifts. Doors recognize you. Opportunities rise to meet you. People show up to support what God already declared possible. Energy rearranges itself around your identity.

This is not magic. This is not coincidence. This is alignment. This is the amazing power of God. Life is not happening *to* you — it is happening *through* you.

Your "**I Am**" is the steering wheel and your belief is the engine. Your vibration is the fuel. And your faith is the road every blessing travels on. You can build a new life at any moment you choose. You can create a new emotional home. You can elevate your frequency. You can speak yourself into peace. You can call forward abundance. You can declare a new identity and watch God breathe life into it. Because the truth is this:

You were never forgotten.

You were never powerless.

You were never empty.

You were never without support.

You simply hadn't remembered who you were. But now you do.! And once you remember, you cannot go back to living as if you are small. Your "**I Am**" will not allow it. God's image within you will not allow it. Your soul will not allow it.

So let this chapter be your turning point, the moment you

stepped into agreement with your divine identity, the moment you stopped calling yourself by your wounds and started calling yourself by your destiny.

This is the moment you finally understand:
When you say "I Am,"
You are activating God within you.
You are shaping your reality.
You are naming your future.
You are remembering your power.
I AM THAT I AM.
And with that knowing, you can boldly declare:
I AM becoming everything God dreamed for me.

There will always be moments when life tries to convince you that you are smaller than your calling. Challenges will arise that whisper old narratives, inviting you back into doubt, fear, or emotional exhaustion. But this is where your spiritual maturity takes the lead. This is where your voice becomes your weapon. This is where your **"I Am"** becomes your grounding force. When you speak with authority, you are not pretending, you are creating, you are choosing the identity your soul already recognizes as true. You are commanding your inner world to align with the Divine blueprint that has always existed within you.

You cannot wait for someone else to validate your power, affirm your worth, or hand you permission to rise. That era is over. From this point forward, you are the narrator of your story and the steward of your destiny, the master of your fate. You decide the tone. You decide the pace. You decide the identity you walk in. Self-motivation is not new age hype; it is spiritual responsibility. Ancient wisdom that our ancestors possessed. It is the daily practice of calling yourself by the highest name God assigned you. And every time you speak "**I Am**" with intention, you are reclaiming territory, internally, emotionally, spiritually, energetically. You are reminding every part of your being that you are not built to bow to circumstances; circumstances bow to the one who remembers their Source.

So use your voice boldly. Speak life into your path. Declare the identity you are stepping into, not the one you survived. When you say "**I Am**," you are not echoing weakness, you are issuing a decree. You are activating spiritual law. You are aligning with the God who breathed identity into existence and placed a piece of Himself inside you. Walk into your life like someone who knows that your words carry creative force, your beliefs shape reality, and your vibration calls forward every blessing assigned to your name. Let this be your truth: **When I speak, I create. When I believe, I become. And when I say "I Am," I awaken the God within me.**

About the Author

SaBrina Fisher Reece is a spiritual teacher, author, entrepreneur, and transformational mindset coach devoted to helping people awaken to their inner power, align with divine truth, and create the life they were designed to live. With decades of experience guiding others through personal growth, faith, mindset, and healing, SaBrina's work bridges spirituality and practical transformation in a way that is both deeply soulful and powerfully accessible.

Her journey has not been one of ease. Marked by early abandonment, loss, trauma, and profound life challenges, SaBrina learned firsthand that survival alone is not the goal—transformation is. Through years of study, spiritual seeking, prayer, meditation, and inner discipline, she discovered that healing is not only possible, it is purposeful. What once threatened to break her became the very fuel that shaped her calling.

SaBrina is the creator of multiple inspirational books and platforms centered on faith, vibration, consciousness, and divine alignment. Her teachings emphasize the power of the mind, the spiritual laws governing manifestation, and the truth that effective prayer is not about begging—it is about partnership with God. She teaches that belief, intention, emotional alignment, and spiritual discipline are the true keys to answered prayers and lasting peace.

Beyond her spiritual work, SaBrina is also a longtime businesswoman and mentor who spent over three decades building successful enterprises while empowering others to find their voice, value, and vision. Her life's work is a living testament to the truth that purpose and prosperity can coexist when guided by integrity, faith, and inner alignment.

At the heart of her message is one unwavering truth: you are not separate from God—you are an expression of God in motion. And when you align your thoughts, emotions, and actions with that truth, miracles move from possibility into experience.

SaBrina currently continues her work through writing, teaching, speaking, and daily spiritual practice—dedicated to reminding others that healing is real, alignment is attainable, and the life you desire is not only possible, it is purposeful.

You can connect with me on:

https://www.facebook.com/BraidQueenSaBrinaReece

https://www.instagram.com/sabrinafisherreece

Also by SaBrina Fisher Reece

SaBrina Fisher Reece's body of work spans personal development, spirituality, emotional wellness, and entrepreneurship. Her books provide clear guidance on mindset mastery, faith-based manifestation, positive identity, effective prayer, emotional balance, sexual-spiritual harmony, and the fundamentals of building and sustaining a small business. Together, her titles offer a comprehensive blueprint for improving both inner life and external success—making her an author dedicated to empowering readers on every level: spiritual, emotional, mental, and practical.

How to Get Exactly
What You Want from God

Mastering the Art of Effective Prayer

SaBrina Fisher Reece

How To Get Exactly What You Want From Good

How to Get Exactly What You Want From God shows you how to pray with results. Inside, you'll learn how to make specific requests, build the faith needed to sustain them, and match your thoughts and emotions to the outcome you want. SaBrina teaches you how to interrupt negative self-talk, eliminate doubt, and step into a mindset that attracts divine answers quickly and clearly. This is your guide to intentional prayer, spiritual alignment, and receiving blessings without hesitation.

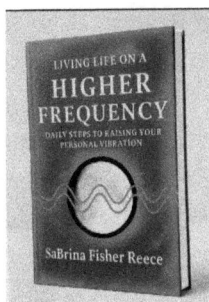

Living Life On A Higher Frequency

Living Life on a Higher Frequency is a spiritually uplifting guide to raising your vibration, shifting your mindset, and aligning with your highest self. Through faith, awareness, and daily intentional practices, SaBrina Fisher Reece empowers readers to live with greater peace, clarity, and purpose.

Your Mind is Magic

Your Mind Is Magic is an empowering guide to mastering your thoughts, reshaping your reality, and unlocking the creative power within you. Through practical tools, spiritual insight, and everyday techniques, SaBrina Fisher Reece teaches how positive thinking, visualization, and intentional belief can transform your life from the inside out.

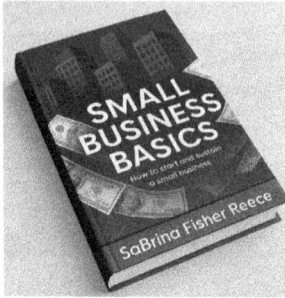

Small Business Basics: How to Start and Sustain a Small Business Small Business Basics is the powerful story of how a young woman with no blueprint, no support, and no safety net built one of Los Angeles' most recognized braid studios—and the step-by-step guide she created so others could rise too.

Through raw honesty and decades of wisdom, SaBrina Fisher Reece reveals the lessons that shaped her journey: how to start before you're ready, how to visualize success, how to market with courage, how to lead with compassion, how to set boundaries, and how to build a business that reflects your purpose—not your past.

This book blends practical business strategies with personal growth, healing, and spiritual insight, reminding readers that entrepreneurship is not just about making money—it's about becoming the strongest version of yourself. If you're ready to build a business rooted in discipline, faith, confidence, and heart, this book will show you the way.